Akathist
to
Saint George of Cernica

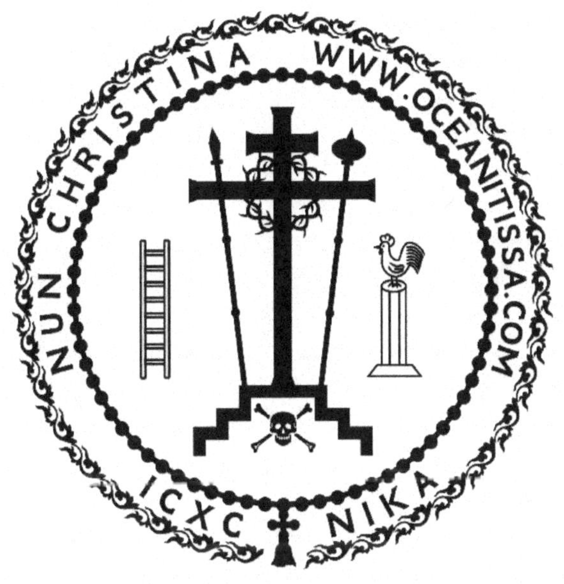

Anna Skoubourdis
Nun Christina

Published by: Virgin Mary of Australia and Oceania 2022 ©
oceanitissa@gmail.com
www.oceanitissa.com.au
Youtube: Nun Christina Oceanitissa

Subscribe to receive updates and Orthodox Christian creative media

www.oceanitissa.com

December 3

Troparion. Tone 4.

Saint Reverend Father George, you proved to be a follower of the Holy Fathers and fulfiller of ascetic virtues, ceaseless suppliant, and innovator of Romanian monasticism. Pray to Christ God to grant us great mercy.

Troparion. Tone 8.

By a flood of tears you made the desert fertile, / and your longing for God brought forth fruits in abundance. / By the radiance of miracles you illumined the whole universe! / O our holy father George, pray to Christ our God to save our souls!

Akathist

Kontakion 1

Let us praise our God-honoring and much zealous Father George, for he, through much toil and hardship as a monk, was worthy of the heavenly Kingdom from Christ God. For this, with humility and faith, let us sing to him from the bottom of our souls: Rejoice, much zealous Reverend Father George!

Ikos 1

Since youth, you wanted the improved life of the monks, Father George, lover of God. That is why you set out on the path of ascetic hardships, entering into the obedience of Saint Paisius of Neamț and, working with righteousness the divine virtues, you made the power of the Holy Spirit dwell in your soul. Marveling at your zeal for spiritual life, we sing to you:

Rejoice, good worker in Christ's vineyard;
Rejoice, lover of the monastic habit;
Rejoice, for your heart was full of grace;
Rejoice, for you have renounced the old man;
Rejoice, for you have put on the new man, built in the image of God;
Rejoice, teacher of the true faith;
Rejoice, fulfiller of Christian virtues;
Rejoice, image of goodness and honor;
Rejoice, for you crucified yourself for Christ since youth;
Rejoice, you who carried the Lord's cross with joy;
Rejoice, disciple of Saint Pious Paisius;
Rejoice, worthy descendant of pious parents;
Rejoice, much zealous Reverend Father George!

Kontakion 2

Through God's care, revealed to you through Saint Hierarch Nicholas, you were appointed to renew the building and community of the Cernica Monastery. And taking the blessing of Christ-loving Metropolitan Gregory, you began the labor of restoring this establishment, singing to God: Alleluia!

Ikos 2

Holy Father, hearing the Savior's call, you accepted the entrusted mission without hesitation and began the spiritual work of restoring the Cernica Monastery and renewing monastic life, for which we praise you, saying:
Rejoice, example of steadiness;
Rejoice, pillar of obedience;
Rejoice, lover of God;
Rejoice, worshiper of the saints;
Rejoice, counselor of monks;
Rejoice, zealous of the desert;
Rejoice, servant of heavenly mysteries;
Rejoice, worker in the Lord's vineyard;
Rejoice, fervent supplicant;
Rejoice, worthy obedient of the Savior's commands;
Rejoice, image of ascetic gentleness;
Rejoice, sleepless guardian in toils and vigils;
Rejoice, much zealous Reverend Father George!

Kontakion 3

Guided by the words of the psalmist saying, 'Cause me to know the way wherein I should walk; For I lift up my soul unto thee,' and tried in the experience of ascetic life, you came together with the teacher Macarius to the place that was revealed to you from above by Saint Nicholas, giving glory to God and singing: Alleluia!

Ikos 3

The power of the Most High descending into your soul,
Venerable Father George, you diligently fulfilled the
commandments of the Gospel of Christ so that your name
quickly became known to the lovers of God around Bucharest,
for which we sing to you:

Rejoice, founder of monastic communities;
Rejoice, guide of pious monks;
Rejoice, you who had Saint Nicholas as your protector;
Rejoice, you who fulfilled the monastic ordinances with love;
Rejoice, follower of Reverend Father Paisius of Neamț;
Rejoice, expeller of seen and unseen enemies from your
monastery;
Rejoice, for the creatures obey your word;
Rejoice, for in everything you have glorified God;
Rejoice, seer of the divine work of created things;
Rejoice, skilled priest and enlightened image;
Rejoice, teacher and spiritual guide of Christians;
Rejoice, embodiment of goodness and humility;
Rejoice, much zealous Reverend Father George!

Kontakion 4

As soon as Metropolitan Gregory blessed you to be the founder
of the community life and steward of the monastic assets from
Cernica, you began, with patience and hope, Pious Father, the
toil of renewal, singing to God: Alleluia!

Ikos 4

Father George, who will not bless you, for you have founded the
Cernica Monastery with wisdom and faith and ordained the
God-pleasing community life. For this, we bring you these
praises:

Rejoice, father, full of divine grace;
Rejoice, for you have dedicated your life to the service of Christ;
Rejoice, for you zealously fulfilled His will;
Rejoice, for you were obedient in everything to your superior;
Rejoice, for you often consulted with him in many things;
Rejoice, bright torch of your disciples;
Rejoice, you who dispelled the darkness of lies;
Rejoice, expeller of hypocritical enemies;
Rejoice, calmer of storms on the sea of life;
Rejoice, for even nature obeys your word;
Rejoice, reconciler of all those who quarreled, separated by the enemy;
Rejoice, steward of holy things;
Rejoice, much zealous Reverend Father George!

Kontakion 5

God-bearing Father, seeing your steadfastness in your spiritual work, the enemy designed many temptations and sorrows for you to doom you; however, after a little while, he was ashamed and left, for you were always singing to God: Alleluia!

Ikos 5

Gifted with the grace of the priesthood, you faithfully served the divine Mysteries of Christ and the Knower of hearts, God, gave you, dear Father, a multitude of disciples and spiritual sons, whom you taught from the edifying word of the Gospel and from the life-giving source of the Holy Spirit, for which we sing to you in wonder:

Rejoice, inhabitant of the desert and unceasing supplicant;
Rejoice, spiritual man and enlightened counselor;
Rejoice, bearer of the grace of the Holy Spirit;
Rejoice, burning candle from the light of Christ;
Rejoice, guiding prayer fire of your disciples;

Rejoice, supporter of the faithful;
Rejoice, follower of the Holy Fathers;
Rejoice, for you have sown the good seed in the hearts of the faithful;
Rejoice, consolation of the sorrowful;
Rejoice, good shepherd of Christ's flock;
Rejoice, abbot, enlightened by the Holy Spirit;
Rejoice, father of fathers of the desert;
Rejoice, much zealous Reverend Father George!

Kontakion 6

Like the buck that seeks to drink from the clear springs of the desert, so your soul, wonderful Father, wanted to rest in the islands of the Holy Mount Athos. But, considering that obedience to the elders of the Church is more holy than your own will, in humility, you cut off your will and, obeying the Holy call, sang to God: Alleluia!

Ikos 6

Loving your nation, Father, although you sought to improve yourself spiritually in other places from the experience of those living in Christ, nevertheless, when you were called to serve the sons of your people from which you came, you responded with joy, for which we sing to you:

Rejoice, follower of the venerable saints of old;
Rejoice, reverend bearer of the gift of humility;
Rejoice, wise in the wisdom of Christ;
Rejoice, conscience of fulfilled duty;
Rejoice, fulfiller of the law and virtues;
Rejoice, intercessor for your nation;
Rejoice, for you have been gifted by Christ with power from above;
Rejoice, you who crucified your cravings along with your passions;

Rejoice, for you have submitted your will to the will of Christ;
Rejoice, for you have raised your mind from earth to heaven;
Rejoice, for you have not attached your heart to fleeting delights;
Rejoice, for you have desired heavenly things all your life;
Rejoice, much zealous Reverend Father George!

Kontakion 7

Father George, purifying the views of the mind through the work of virtues, you reached the state of dispassion and, contemplating Christ unceasingly in your heart, sang to God: Alleluia!

Ikos 7

You made yourself a living icon of prayer, fasting, and vigils for your disciples, and the news of your angelic life spread throughout Wallachia. For this, we sing to you:

Rejoice, for your being was full of the Trinity;
Rejoice, mind full of humble contemplation;
Rejoice, for you have cleansed your life of sins;
Rejoice, chosen flower planted in the garden of the Mother of God;
Rejoice, rose with petals beautified by the light of Christ;
Rejoice, for your heart spreads the fragrance of spiritual love;
Rejoice, father full of divine grace;
Rejoice, for the enemies could not destroy your steadfastness in prayer;
Rejoice, you who, by the call of the Spirit, brought heaven down to earth;
Rejoice, good example to the zealous believers;
Rejoice, follower of Saint Nicholas in helping your neighbor;
Rejoice, for you pray for the monastic order together with the Holy Hierarch Calinic;
Rejoice, much zealous Reverend Father George!

Kontakion 8

Reverend Father, your teachings have spread throughout the
land of our country, and the multitude of believers, coming to
you, drink as if from a grace-giving and blessed spring, thanking
God and singing: Alleluia!

Ikos 8

You defended the Orthodox faith, followed the ascetic path, and
adorned with virtues and holy hope, you reached the Benevolent
God, Reverend Father, for, receiving the unfading crown of
glory, you moved from the ephemeral to the heavenly. For this,
we sing you this hymn:

Rejoice, for by the grace of God and by hardships, you have
gained heaven;
Rejoice, for patience was your anchor and strength;
Rejoice, for Christ has crowned you in heaven;
Rejoice, for you have entered the company of the Holy Saints;
Rejoice, pearl of the Romanian saints;
Rejoice, for your name is written in the book of life;
Rejoice, for from this earth you were planted in the garden of
heaven;
Rejoice, for you see the face of Christ whom you loved;
Rejoice, for we - your descendants - keep your memory alive;
Rejoice, for your departure to heaven has filled us with joy;
Rejoice, you who spend eternity in the Most Holy Trinity;
Rejoice, for you always rejoice in the light of divinity;
Rejoice, much zealous Reverend Father George!

Kontakion 9

Your body, full of the fragrance of virtues, was placed in the Cernica Monastery, which you built with so much effort, along with those of other pious and ascetic fathers, and your soul dwells in the heavenly abodes, singing to God: Alleluia!

Ikos 9

Although you have passed from this life to eternal life, Reverend Father George, you have not left those who struggle with the troubles and temptations of this world, for you always intercede with the Most Merciful God for those who sing:

Rejoice, Pious Father, glorified founder;
Rejoice, fervent supplicant for the Romanian nation;
Rejoice, the praise of the Orthodox and the joy of the monks;
Rejoice, bearer of the heavenly crown;
Rejoice, tower of Christianity and pillar of the Church;
Rejoice, our bravery to God;
Rejoice, servant of Christ and friend of the angels;
Rejoice, spiritual flower opened in the hope of fruit;
Rejoice, good seed sown in the fruitful soil;
Rejoice, enlightener of monks and guide of the needy;
Rejoice, knower of the mysteries of God;
Rejoice, tireless in spreading the holy writings;
Rejoice, much zealous Reverend Father George!

Kontakion 10

The groups of ascetic monks and the multitude of humble Christians have you as a light-bearing torch, emanating a good fragrance to all and healing those who lovingly honor and worship your holy relics as they thank God for having been given such a gift, singing: Alleluia!

Ikos 10

Praising your toils, Reverend Father, and honoring your holy relics, we joyfully sing your coronation in heaven, praying with faith that you help us in the time of temptations and dangers that surround us in this world so that we can sing to you:

Rejoice, bearer of the gift of healing;
Rejoice, doer of miracles for the faithful;
Rejoice, source of healing and healer of pain;
Rejoice, quick helper of the afflicted;
Rejoice, ray of sunshine for the pious people;
Rejoice, spiritual harbor for the weary;
Rejoice, shining torch in the night of temptations;
Rejoice, morning star rising in the darkness of troubles;
Rejoice, friend and householder of God;
Rejoice, suppliant to the Mother of God;
Rejoice, interpreter of divine mysteries;
Rejoice, you who live with the angels;
Rejoice, much zealous Reverend Father George!

Kontakion 11

You pour comfort and peace of mind into the hearts of the faithful, those who honor your memory with love, much zealous Saint Reverend George, and thanking God, sing: Alleluia!

Ikos 11

Holy Father, being brave before the Merciful God Whom you loved, we beseech you, those who commemorate you with love, to deliver us from hardships, dangers, and needs, so that we may sing to you:

Rejoice, man of God and faithful servant;
Rejoice, sapling loaded with the fruits of the Holy Spirit;
Rejoice, sweet consolation of the monks;

Rejoice, strength of the faithful in temptations;
Rejoice, protector of monasteries and awakening to spiritual life;
Rejoice, image of meekness and example of humility;
Rejoice, together with the Holy Great Martyr George;
Rejoice, servant of truth and man of justice;
Rejoice, discoverer of things to come;
Rejoice, glorified body and deified soul;
Rejoice, fragrant incense and ever-burning candle;
Rejoice, voice listened to by Christ, your Master;
Rejoice, much zealous Reverend Father George!

Kontakion 12

God Almighty, wanting to give our righteous Church a sign of
His presence, chose you, Reverend Father George, to be our
unquenchable light and fountain of grace. For this, we sing to
Him with gratitude: Alleluia!

Ikos 12

Be a wall of defense against temptations and a fervent supplicant
for us, Reverend Father, for, having courage in front of the
Merciful God, we hope that you will always protect us against
the evils of this world and the arrows of the cunning one so that
we can bring you these praises:

Rejoice, father of orphans and supporter of the oppressed;
Rejoice, feeder of the hungry;
Rejoice, defender of the oppressed;
Rejoice, wealth of the poor;
Rejoice, harbor of the troubled;
Rejoice, bringer of abundance;
Rejoice, banisher of drought;
Rejoice, protector of widows and the elderly
Rejoice, counselor of monks;
Rejoice, fervent supplicant for our souls;
Rejoice, destroyer of temptations;

Rejoice, the intercessor of our salvation;
Rejoice, much zealous Reverend Father George!

Kontakion 13

O zealous one, Reverend Father Gheorghe, receive from us, the unworthy, this little prayer, take it to Christ God and ask him to deliver us from all the troubles and temptations of earthly life, to protect us from the torment that awaits us for our sins and make us worthy of the Kingdom of Heaven so that we can sing with love: Alleluia! (*Repeat this kontakion three times.*)

Repeat Ikos 1 and Kontakion 1.

Ikos 1

Since youth, you wanted the improved life of the monks, Father George, lover of God. That is why you set out on the path of ascetic hardships, entering into the obedience of Saint Paisius of Neamț and, working with righteousness the divine virtues, you made the power of the Holy Spirit dwell in your soul. Marveling at your zeal for spiritual life, we sing to you:

Rejoice, good worker in Christ's vineyard;
Rejoice, lover of the monastic habit;
Rejoice, for your heart was full of grace;
Rejoice, for you have renounced the old man;
Rejoice, for you have put on the new man, built in the image of God;
Rejoice, teacher of the true faith;
Rejoice, fulfiller of Christian virtues;
Rejoice, image of goodness and honor;
Rejoice, for you crucified yourself for Christ since youth;
Rejoice, you who carried the Lord's cross with joy;
Rejoice, disciple of Saint Pious Paisius;
Rejoice, worthy descendant of pious parents;
Rejoice, much zealous Reverend Father George!

Kontakion 1

Let us praise our God-honoring and much zealous Father George, for he, through much toil and hardship as a monk, was worthy of the heavenly Kingdom from Christ God. For this, with humility and faith, let us sing to him from the bottom of our souls: Rejoice, much zealous Reverend Father George!

Dismissal prayer.

Biography

Saint George was born in 1730, and became a monk on Mount Athos when he was a young man. He was a disciple of Saint Paisius Velichkovsky (November 15) who was then the igumen of Vatopedi Monastery.

Since the skete at Cernica had been deserted for almost thirty years, Metropolitan Gregory II of Wallachia asked Elder George to revive monastic life there according to the Athonite Typikon.

Saint George's efforts at Cernica were so successful that Metropolitan Philaret II also entrusted him with leading the Caldarushani Monastery, which he guided until his death. Life at both monasteries followed the Athonite-Paisian hesychastic tradition.

Saint George was glorified by the Romanian Orthodox Church in 2005. His holy relics are in the Cernica Monastery, where they are venerated by the faithful.

Books published by Nun Christina Oceanitissa:

The collective works of St Nektarios of Aegina.
The Philokalia 5: The full text in English.
The collective works of Elder Cleopa.
The Anacreontic Poems by Saint Sophronius Patriarch of Jerusalem.
The Life of Saint Paul of Thebes the First Hermit.
The Devil: The Cause of Sin by Saint John of Kronstadt.
Faith and the Orthodox Church by Saint John of Kronstadt.
The Monastic Rule of Saint Pachomius the Great.
Supplicatory Canon and Akathist to St Paisios.
Supplicatory Canon and Akathist to St Porphyrios.
Supplicatory Canon and Akathist to St George.
Supplicatory Canon and Akathist to St Anastasia.
Supplicatory Canon and Akathist to St Anna.
Supplicatory Canon and Akathist to St John the Russian.
Supplicatory Canon and Akathist to St Ephraim of Nea Makri.
Supplicatory Canon and Akathist to St John Maximovitch.
Supplicatory Canon and Akathist to St Dimitri.
Supplicatory Canon and Akathist to St Joseph the Hesycast.
Supplicatory Canon and Akathist to St Luke the Surgeon.
Supplicatory Canon and Akathist to St John the Baptist.
The Way of a Pilgrim.
Conversation with a Grieving Man by St Dimitri of Rostov.
The Inner Man by St Dimitri of Rostov.
Orthodox Prayer Book.
Daily Orthodox Prayer book.